Love

Kenneth E. Hagin

CHAPTER 1

❧

Love Your Enemies

*But I say unto you, Love your enemies,
bless them that curse you, do good to them
that hate you, and pray for them which
despitefully use you, and persecute you.*

—Matthew 5:44

This verse tells us what and whom to pray for. It's Jesus talking. He's saying, *"Love your enemies. . . ."* It's easy to love your friends, isn't it? Yes, they're so lovely. Enemies are not lovely, though. They don't act lovely. They don't always treat you lovely, do they?

Did you notice what Jesus said to do? *Love, bless, do good,* and *pray.* If you do these things, you're going to make it.

"But I say unto you, Love your enemies. . . ." How can you do that? You can't do it unless you've been born again and the love of God is in you. Natural man can't do that—it's impossible. But the Bible says that *". . . the love of God is shed abroad in our hearts*—not our heads—*by the Holy Ghost."* What kind of love? The God-kind of love.

The Bible tells us that God loved us while we were yet His enemies. And we can love just like God loves, because the love of God has been shed abroad in our hearts. So love your enemies! *"Bless them that curse you, do good to them that hate you. . . ."* If you know somebody hates you, find something good that you can do for them. Buy them a birthday gift and give it to them. Send them a special offering.

A woman Bible teacher faced this situation in her hometown. Another minister there didn't like women preachers to begin with. Some people because of their *religious* upbringing—I didn't say Christian or New Testament—don't believe in women preachers. And I think some men just don't particularly like women, anyway.

So this man persecuted her, even referring to her by name.

She prayed, "Lord, I am not going to let it bother me. What could I do for him?" She took up an offering and sent it to him. She realized his congregation was struggling, trying to pay for their church. Well, it wasn't long until he had her over there speaking in his church—preaching right in the pulpit!

Do good! *"Do good to them that hate you."* Find out something that you can do for them. Send them an offering. Hallelujah, it works—and besides that, it's the right thing to do and it's in the Bible.

"*. . . Pray for them which despitefully use you, and persecute you.*" It's easier from the natural standpoint—if you want to let the flesh dominate you—to fight them and answer them back. But I learned a long time ago that the best thing in the world you can do is to start praying for them.

Somebody will say, "Yeah, but you don't understand—you just don't understand what all they've done."

An example of walking in love is the way Polly Wigglesworth treated her husband, Smith, before he got to preaching.

Smith related the story to Brother Stanley Frodsham, and he wrote it down.

Smith said, "I owe my ministry to my wife (of course, God comes first). There was a time my plumbing business was prospering and I grew cold. I didn't go to church much—I backslid, in other words.

"And when you backslide, you get cantankerous. So I said to my wife, 'You're up at that church all the time. You might as well move your bed up there!'

"'Well, no,' she said. 'Smith, I'm not up there all the time—I'm only up there about three times a week. I do not neglect you or the children, and you know that.'"

Some people know just enough Scripture to be devilish. Smith replied, "Well, I know the Bible says that the man is the head of the house—'Wives, obey your husbands'—so I'm telling you, don't you go to church anymore!"

Polly said, "Now, Smith, you are my husband, and whatever you say here in the house goes. But you're not my Lord. Jesus is my Lord, and He said go, so I'm going to church. Goodbye."

He said, "The next time you go, I'm going to lock you out!" (Evidently she didn't have a key to the house.) So he locked her out.

She sat out on the porch all night. He went downstairs the next morning, unlocked the door, and found Polly all wrapped up (it must have been cool), huddled against the door. She almost fell into the kitchen as he opened the door.

Smith related, "She just bounded up, smiling and laughing, and said, 'Dear, what would you like for breakfast?' She acted like nothing had happened and was happy and loving."

Polly prepared her husband's favorite breakfast, and then Smith felt convicted, of course.

He said later, "If it hadn't been for her, I'd never have made it." He became a great man of God and was mightily used.

❧

CHAPTER 2

New Testament Examples

Jesus is our example. Notice that it is He who is speaking in Matthew 5:44. The Bible tells us that right on the cross, Jesus prayed for the very people who crucified Him. He said, *"Father, forgive them; for they know not what they do"* (Luke 23:34).

Someone will want to argue, "Yeah, but that was Jesus—He could do that."

But the love of God has been shed abroad in our hearts.

Did you ever notice what Stephen, the first martyr, said as he was dying?

ACTS 7:59–60

59 And they stoned Stephen, calling upon God, and saying, Lord Jesus, receive my spirit.

60 And he kneeled down, and cried with a loud voice, Lord, lay not this sin to their charge. And when he had said this, he fell asleep.

Now that's love, isn't it? People were beating him to death, and he was praying for them.

Did you ever notice what Peter said over in First Peter 3, writing to the Church under the inspiration of the Holy Spirit?

1 PETER 3:8-10

8 Finally, be ye all of one mind, having compassion one of another, love as brethren, be pitiful, be courteous:

9 Not rendering evil for evil, or railing for railing but contrariwise blessing; knowing that ye are thereunto called, that ye should inherit a blessing.

10 For he that will love life, and see good days, let him refrain his tongue from evil, and his lips that they speak no guile.

Notice the blessing he's saying you can inherit (verse 9). The same Greek word translated "compassion" in verse 8 also can be translated "mercy"; for example, "be ye all of one mind, having mercy one of another." Remember, he said we weren't to render evil for evil.

Verse 11 continues, *"Let him eschew evil, and do good; let him seek peace, and ensue it."*

I've had this work for me among my own kinfolks. Once while I was busy holding two services a day in a large city, my brother Dub came to see me. He offered to take care of some family business for me in another town, and I agreed.

When he returned to see me, he reported that he hadn't been able to complete the business because some relatives had mistrusted his motives and had treated him badly. In fact, they had cussed him out.

Dub said, "Don't you go there. They'll whip you!"

I said, "Dub, bless your heart, you're just a baby Christian. You don't know how to handle them."

"Well, don't you go!"

I said, "I have to go attend to the business. The Greater One is in me. He who is in me is bigger than the devil in them. The Lord who is in me is bigger than the hate that's in them. Greater! Greater! You just don't know how to put it to work yet."

So I went to this town and right away one relative heard I was visiting and called me outside to talk. I never will forget it.

I went out and stood on the back steps. This woman walked toward me, ranting and raving, words running like water out of a faucet. I don't know to this day much of what she said—I didn't pay too much attention.

She got right up to me. I was standing two steps above her, looking down at her. She looked up into my face, her eyes blazing. She was virtually cursing.

"Nobody's going to beat us out of anything," she raved. "I'll tell you that much right now!" She went on and on like this.

I never said a word. I talked softly to myself. I stood there and meditated, *The*

Greater One is in me. Greater is the love that's in me than the hatred, greed, and selfishness that's in her.

Then I got to thinking about it: *Well, that poor dear can't help acting that way—I know she's acting awful, but she can't help acting that way. She's got the nature of the devil in her.*

She was going on and on. I guess a look of pity crossed my face, but I never said a word. Suddenly she looked up in my face and came to a stop. Her mouth was flapping, but nothing came out.

She grabbed my hand, kissed it, and got down on her knees. She said, "O my God, Ken, put your hand on my head and pray. Oh, I need prayer. O my God, we all need prayer! Put your hand on my head!"

I never had said a word. I had just looked at her and had loved her. You know, you can *see* love. I never said, "I love you" or "Jesus loves you." I just looked at her in compassion and pity. (I think sometimes a look can be more powerful than words.) This look melted her.

I got my business transacted among my relatives and the ones who had been the most difficult were just as nice as they could be.

Greater is He—*greater, greater*!

CHAPTER 3

Love's Rewards

I'm in my 59th year of divine health. I'm not bragging on me; I'm bragging on Jesus. I'm certainly not opposed to medical science. Thank God for medical science. Thank God for doctors; especially Christian doctors.

I remember back before I knew there were other people who believed in divine healing—Pentecostal people and so on. I was Baptist, and I'd seen the prayer of faith, Mark 11:23 and 24, on the bed of sickness. I had prayed it for myself and was healed.

One night I was visiting some more good Baptist people in their home. (You've got to remember that this was back in the '30s, and doctors made house calls then.)

The head of the house had become ill, but when I went to visit them, I did not know he was sick. When I got there, I found they already had called the doctor.

He was a good Baptist doctor. He was a saved man. He didn't know anything about the baptism in the Holy Spirit or much about divine healing. Before he got there, the family had asked me to pray. Even though I was just a teenager, they knew I was a preacher, so I prayed.

Those were Depression days. The family was greatly concerned. The breadwinner of the home was sick, and it looked like it might be quite serious. He had a job. You were fortunate if you had a job in those Depression days. The streets were full of men standing around with no work—nothing.

I think the devil gave the family visions of losing everything they had, going hungry, and being on relief.

When the doctor came, I think he could see the concern written all over them. The first thing this Baptist doctor did, before he ever examined the man, was take him by the hand and say, "Dear brother (they were members of the same church), look to the Lord. Just relax and look to the Lord. He's the Healer; I'm not. I'm going to do what I can to help you, but He's the Great Physician."

By quietly saying those words, it seemed the whole atmosphere of that room changed. And that look of anxiety on the family's faces just seemed to disappear as they rested in the Lord. The man was all right in two or three days.

This Christian doctor was in his early 70s. He was so calm and gentle, and he spoke with such confidence: "Look to the Lord! Rest in Him. We'll do what we can, but the Lord is the great Healer. He can work when nobody else can." That's what the Baptist doctor said. He'd found that out through the years. He could speak with confidence. And it brought peace, rest, and confidence to that family.

I believe in good doctors; especially Christian doctors. And if I needed a doctor,

I'd go to one. If I needed to. But I haven't even had a headache since 1933.

The last headache I had was in August of 1933. I haven't had as much as an aspirin in 60 years. But if I needed to go to the doctor, I'd go.

In recent years, I've sent some people to the doctor and paid their bill myself. I've even bought medicine for them, because I realized they needed it.

I don't want to bring you into bondage. If you have had to go to the doctor, you may not have known what I knew to begin with. But I know if you are going to walk in health, you are going to have to walk close to God. You're going to have to do what He said here, and walk in love. I'll show you how I learned it.

The verse that brought me off the bed of sickness was Mark 11:24:

MARK 11:24

24 Therefore I say unto you, What things soever ye desire, when ye pray, believe that ye receive them, and ye shall have them.

The very next verse begins, *"And when ye stand praying, forgive, if ye have ought against any. . . ."* (v. 25).

You see, you have to love your enemies. You have to bless them that curse you. You have to do good to them that don't do good to you. You are not walking in forgiveness unless you do. And God not only *forgives;* He *forgets.*

Any number of times, just like anybody else, I've been tempted not to forgive, but I refuse to let the least bit of animosity—the least bit of ill will—the least bit of wrong feeling—get in me. In fact, if people begin to talk about me, I start praying for them. I wake up in the morning and say, "God bless dear Brother So-and-so. Now, I don't know what he meant by what he said—that's between him and You—but I know You want to bless him. I pray that his ministry will be blessed. I pray that You'll give him divine guidance and direction. I pray that You'll use him and make him a blessing to others."

I don't want to see any minister miss it, do you? Often people don't know what they're doing. Jesus said of the very ones who crucified Him, "Forgive them. They know not what they do."

By the time I was in the second grade, I was mad at the whole world. I felt like I'd been cheated in life.

Our home was divided. My oldest brother, Dub, had to go live with some kinfolks, and I lived with others. We didn't get to see each other very often.

He and I made a solemn pact when I was 9 and he was 11 that when we were grown, we were going to kill our daddy for what he had done to our mother. We knew we couldn't do it then, but we knew we could when we got grown. And we'd have done it, too. It wouldn't have solved anything, but we intended to do it.

The only thing that kept him from getting killed was my getting saved. Then I talked Dub out of it.

I couldn't take up for myself like Dub could. He was big—he was over 6 feet tall when he was a 16-year-old boy—and he wouldn't take anything off of anybody. I've seen Dub at 17 take on four grown men at once and whip all four right there in my hometown of McKinney, Texas.

We both grew up twisted in mind and with a chip on our shoulders. If some of the kinfolks did Dub wrong, he'd whip them. I couldn't start anything because I had a heart condition. If they did me wrong, I'd say to myself, *Well now, that's it. I'll never speak to them again.* I marked them off my list and gave them the silent treatment. I'd turn my back on them, or even cross the street in the middle of the block to keep from meeting them.

But then I got born again while an invalid. The Bible says, *". . . the love of God is shed abroad in our hearts by the Holy Ghost . . ."* (Rom. 5:5).

It wasn't too many weeks after I was healed at age 17 that one of my kinfolks did me an injustice. I remember I said to myself when this happened, *I'll give them the old treatment. I won't speak to them or have anything to do with them anymore!* (I didn't have my mind renewed yet with the Word of God.)

The next day after I said that, I was walking downtown in the business district and I saw this person coming toward me. The thought crossed my mind, *I'll look in this store window and turn my back on them.* Another thought flashed across my mind: *I'll cross the street here in the middle of the block so I won't have to meet them.*

But then something rose up inside me. The Bible says, *"the love of Christ constraineth us..."* (2 Cor. 5:14). That love was in my spirit. I didn't have to let it dominate me—I could have let my natural human reasoning and flesh dominate me—but thank God I let that love rise up in me.

20

Instead of turning against those folks, I went to meet them right on the street. I reached out my hand to them, shook hands with them, and told them that I loved them. I said with tears, "I'm praying for you, and I want you to know something: If it would help you any, I would get down on my knees right here on the street and kiss your feet."

When I said that, they started crying, "O my God, O my God—ohhh! Forgive me. Forgive me. I've done you an injustice. Forgive me. I shouldn't have said what I said!"

Love never fails. I began to walk in love.

To fellowship with God, to walk with God, to walk in God's realm, to walk in the Spirit, we must walk in divine love, for God is love, the Bible says.

To walk in love means to walk in the Spirit, because love is a fruit of the Spirit.

When I was born again, God became my Father. He's a love God. I'm a love child of a love God. I'm born of God, and God is love. So I'm born of love. The nature of God is in me, and the nature of God is love.

21

We can't say we don't have His divine love, because the Bible says we have it. Everyone in the family of God has it, or else they're not in the family. Now, they may not be exercising it, but they have it.

The first fruit of this recreated, born-again human spirit, according to the Bible, is love. Jesus said in John 13:35, *"By this shall all men know that ye are my disciples, if ye have love one to another."*

In the 34th verse He says, *"That ye love one another; as I have loved you...."* He loved us while we were yet unlovely. He loved us while we were yet sinners. He loved us while we were yet His enemies.

Now think about this: If God loved us with so great a love when we were sinners, think how He loves His children! Glory to God!

The only commandment Jesus gave us was the commandment of love, and He put the love of God in our hearts. As we saw, Romans 5:5 says, *"The love of God is shed abroad in our hearts by the Holy Ghost."*

I think, however, that this love business gets all mixed up. Often when you talk about love, people think about natural human love. We hear a lot today about natural human love, but there is no love in all of this old world like the love of God. *Natural human love is selfish.*

I've heard people say that a mother's love is akin to the love of God, and I thought that myself when I was walking more in the soul realm than in the spirit realm, but I found out that that isn't true. As a rule, a mother's love is a natural love, and it's selfish: "*My* baby," "Oh, I love *my* children," "*I* love them."

Did you ever notice in life that mothers-in-law rarely have trouble with sons-in-law? Usually it's always with daughters-in-law. You see, that mother is selfish. That's her boy, and she doesn't think there's any girl in the world good enough for "*my* boy." (And that happens even with born-again, Spirit filled people.)

The reason mothers-in-law have trouble with daughters-in-law is because they don't always walk in love; that is, in divine love. The love of God is in our hearts. We should let that love dominate us. If we'd learn to walk in love and let love dominate us, it would make a difference in our lives. It would cure the ills in our homes.

I'm going to state something that's hard, but it's true: This kind of love has never been to a divorce court, and it never will. It was natural, human love that went there.

God wants us to grow. And, thank God, we can grow in love, because love's a fruit, and fruit grows.

By showing the right spirit and loving people, you'll reap rich rewards.

CHAPTER 4

Love Is the Better Way

Some time ago I was at a ministers' meeting. The leading Full Gospel leaders and ministers of the nation were there. I taught for about 30 to 45 minutes on the subject of "Faith," and then let them ask me questions about faith for another hour and a half.

After I finished, minister after minister came to me and hugged my neck, saying tearfully, "Brother Hagin, I want you to forgive me. Why, my God, I believe everything just exactly like you do. I agree with you one hundred percent. The trouble was I heard some things third- or fourth-hand. What you believe was misrepresented to me."

Since then, one of our students said, "My mother just called and said our pastor got up

Sunday morning and said, 'Folks, I must apologize. I have to do this publicly because I called a man's name publicly. I said this faith message is all wrong, and I mentioned Kenneth Hagin's name. But since seeing him and talking to him, I want everybody to know that I believe just like he does. I want to encourage you to read his books. I want to ask you to forgive me.'"

I'll tell you—love is the best way. Often people don't mean to miss it; they just don't know better. So I'm not going to get all flustered by it and miss the blessing. I've never had any problem with fellow ministers. I love them. I don't talk about them. If somebody else comes and talks to me about a minister, I say, "Well, let's pray for him."

I'm not going around peddling gossip. Somebody will say, "What if it's so?" I'm still not going to do it, because they may have missed it. Who of us hasn't missed it? Do you know anybody who hasn't?

Perhaps they've gotten it all straightened out after they missed it. If I were going around peddling gossip about them, it would ruin their ministry. I refuse to do that. I refuse to tell tales. I don't have a slop bucket for an ear. I'm not going to let somebody pour a bunch of slop in my ear. It'll affect your health if you do.

So I never have any problems with fellow ministers. They may have something against me, but if they do, I don't know it.

I remember one church I pastored. The church was full and running over when I left. God was a blessing. But my daddy-in-law came back from a visit down there and asked me, "What's happened?" I said, "I don't know. Why?"

He said, "We went down there to visit on Sunday night. I counted, and counting my wife and me, there were 40 of us—preacher and everybody—just a little bunch sitting down front. The building used to be full."

"I don't know what happened," I said.

A few days later, I had to go to that town on business. I didn't visit any church members, because I knew the church was having problems. (Four o'clock in the morning would often find me on my knees praying for that pastor.)

I thought I'd drive by the parsonage, because I knew that if the pastor saw me driving around town, he might suspect I'd been visiting some of his members.

I sat in my car and he came outside. I told him I had had some business in town and thought I'd stop by and see him. I asked how things were going. He was angry. "Things aren't right!" he said. He started to blame me for all of his problems.

He said the people weren't paying their tithes. He thought they were giving me the money. "You've been coming around here collecting tithes and creating problems," he said. Oh, he was mad! He even reached into the car and grabbed my necktie. I thought he was going to pull me out of the car.

This was during World War II. I had had a tire problem and had just gotten a new tire. The lug wrench for the tire was right under the driver's seat. I was tempted—O dear God, I was tempted! I even reached down and put my hand on the wrench.

Then I imagined the headlines: "Full Gospel Pastor Knocks Another Full Gospel Pastor on the Head" (or maybe even killed him).

So I said with tears, "Dear brother, dear brother. God is my eternal witness, day before yesterday at four o'clock in the morning I was on my bare knees on the cold linoleum floor praying for you. I was right down on my face, saying, 'God bless dear Brother So-and-so.' I know problems exist here; I pastored this church."

Every time I opened my mouth, he jumped like I had hit him with a whip.

Then he started sobbing, "My God, Brother Hagin! My God, dear brother! Dear brother, forgive me! I—I—I knew everything I said wasn't right. I had to blame my failure

29

on somebody. My God, I just didn't handle it right. I didn't do right—I know I didn't. I've run half the people off. I've divided the church. You were a success, and I wasn't, and I was blaming you. Forgive me. Will you forgive me?"

I said, "Sure, I forgive you."

We hugged one another's neck. Isn't that better than fighting? He's my friend to this day. I'm his.

I know from experience, dear friends, if you're going to walk in health, you're going to have to walk in love and pray for those who persecute you and despitefully use you. Pray for them: That's the best way in the world to overcome the problem.

Yes, I've sometimes reached the point where I wanted to let the flesh dominate me. As I said, I wanted to knock that preacher in the head when he accused me of stealing, but I won't let the flesh dominate me.

Notice the Scripture says, *"Not rendering evil for evil, or railing for railing."* If they "rail" on you, don't rail on them, *"but contrariwise blessing."* Blessing, blessing, blessing, blessing.

I remember an evangelist we had once. Bless his heart, he created more problems in the short length of time he was with us than the devil could have! (The devil had been working on my church for two years and hadn't succeeded, but that preacher succeeded in two weeks.)

He shouldn't have done this—it was none of his business—but he'd go out during the day, look up church members, talk to them, and try to find out everything he could to start problems.

I was tempted—oh, I was tempted—to get back at him. Something said to me, "If I were you, I'd never take up another offering for him. Just wait till Sunday night and say, 'This is Brother So-and-so's offering. Pass the plate and don't say much about it, so he won't get much.'" You see, that would be railing for railing and evil for evil.

I said, "Just for that, Mr. Devil, I'm going to take him up an offering every night." And I did! I gave him twice as much. I blessed him. When the devil came after me again, I said, "If you don't shut up, I'm going to take up *two* offerings a night for the evangelist!"

He hushed right away. He didn't want any preacher to get two offerings a night. So the evangelist went away with a "good taste in his mouth," and I'd rather it be that way.

That has something to do with prayer, and it has something to do with faith. Whom are you to pray for? All the brethren you know who treat you well? No, *"pray for them which despitefully use you, and persecute you."* Are you doing it? If you'll get started, it will help you in other areas.